DISCARD

Beauty Pageants

A Miss International
Beauty Pageant
Winner

Beauty Pageants
Tiaras, Roses, and Runways

By Judy Alter

A First Book

Franklin Watts

A DIVISION OF GROLIER PUBLISHING

New York   London   Hong Kong   Sydney
Danbury, Connecticut

The author wishes to thank Griff O'Neil, founder and president of the International Pageant Association, for assistance in providing printed material.

Photographs ©: AP/Wide World Photos: 30, 38; Archive Photos: 8 (Reuters/Jeff Christensen), 25, 28, 33, 47, 53; Corbis-Bettmann: 23, 27, 32 top right, 37, 51; Gamma-Liaison: 54 (Evan Agostini), 43 (D. Barritt), 13 (S. Kogure), 59 (N. Hosaka), 2, 45, 56 (George Rose), 19 (Tait Selwin), 15, 17 (Taylor/Fabricius), 41 (Eric Vandeville); Reuters/Corbis-Bettmann: 49; Shooting Star Photography: 11, 40, 42; UPI/Corbis-Bettmann: cover, 10, 14, 21, 22, 29, 31, 32 top left, 32 bottom, 35, 36.
Author Photograph ©: Smiley's Studio, Fort Worth, Texas

Library of Congress Cataloging-in-Publication Data

Alter, Judy
    Beauty Pageants: tiaras, roses, and runways / Judy Alter.
        p. cm. — (A First book)
    Includes bibliographical references and index.
    Summary: Examines beauty pageants past and present, their contestants, and their possible future.
    ISBN 0-531-20253-4 (lib.bdg.)   0-531-15874-8 (pbk.)
     1. Beauty contests—United States—Juvenile literature. [1. Beauty contests.
  I. Title. II. Series.
  HQ1220.U5A47 1997
  791.6—dc20   96-41100
                                        CIP
                                        AC

Contents

one
"THERE SHE IS —
MISS
AMERICA!"

Every September, to the background of the now famous song that begins: "There She Is — Miss America," a young woman wearing a sparkling crown and carrying a bouquet of flowers comes to the center of the stage. She walks down a 125-foot runway to the enthusiastic applause of a large Atlantic City crowd, watched by an even greater television audience. Having demonstrated not only beauty but also talent, education, and a concern for others, she is more than merely a beauty queen. Some people go as far as to say that she is the ideal young woman in America, the best of the best.

The pageant has never been without critics. Some claim that Miss America is just a cheerleader and that young women with real talent have no need to enter such contests — and don't. Those who enter, say critics, are willing to mold themselves into a pattern that has long been

The newly crowned Miss America 1996, Tara Dawn Holland of Kansas, waves to the audience as she walks down the Atlantic City runway.

set. In a contest which claims to encourage individuality, Miss America contestants, say some, all look alike and all seem to act alike.

As she walks down the runway, Miss America is making her first public appearance, claiming the crown that she has just been voted by a panel of judges. The sparkling tiara is placed on her head by the outgoing queen. Ahead lies a busy year of public appearances and travel. But also ahead are college scholarships, television opportunities, and an almost unlimited future.

When most of us hear "beauty pageant," we think of the Miss America Pageant. Although it is the oldest and the best known pageant, there are about 35,000 pageants each year at the local, state, and national level. They attract some three million contestants. The United States has two other major pageant systems. Both GuyRex's Miss United States and the Miss USA competitions are like the Miss America system in that local and state pageants feed into a national contest. Both of those pageants, however, lead to international competitions — Miss United States enters the Miss World contest, and Miss USA enters the Miss Universe pageant. The Miss America winner does not go on to another level of competition. The Miss America pageant is the final event of that pageant system.

The emotional climax of a Miss Black Teenage America Beauty Pageant

Other pageants celebrate almost anything you can think of. No matter what your size, shape, age, or ethnic origin, there's a pageant for you! The Miss Black America Pageant draws attention to the achievements of African-American women; another celebrates young women of Native American descent. There's the Mrs. America Pageant for married women, the Miss Teen

Pageant for women under eighteen, and a variety of product titles, such as Miss Cotton or Miss Wool. For large women, there's the Large Lovely Lady Pageant; petites can compete for the title of Tiny Miss United States. The Beauties of America contest has age categories for everyone from young girls to grandmothers.

Contestants for the Miss Teen USA title take a break during rehearsals for the pageant.

two

TRAINING FOR A
PAGEANT

Pageant competition starts at an early age—well over half of all entrants are children, some less than a year old. The Regal Miss Pageant contest has age categories from birth to eighteen; then there's the Teddy Bear Baby Pageant, the Cinderella Pageant, and many others. These children's pageants are often called youth development programs—they prepare youngsters for the bigger pageants that they may enter in their late teens.

At the other end of the age scale is the competition for the title of Mrs. Senior. At one recent state contest in Missouri, entertainment was presented by a tap dance troupe named Fabulous Feet. Its members ranged in age from sixty-four to seventy-seven years.

Pageantry is now such big business that the industry—called "the pageant, self-enhancement, and talent industry"—created a watchdog agency, the International Pageant Association, in the early 1990s. The IPA sanctions, or approves, pageants that meet its standards, much as professional organizations supervise tennis, golf, football, and other sports activities. The IPA standards call for professional behavior by staff members, prompt awarding of prizes promised in promotional material, the same judging standards for all contestants, and a twenty-four-point code of ethics to which pageant directors must agree.

In recent years, pageants have been attacked on television and in newspapers for dishonest practices and for

The International Pageant Association sanctions state and local as well as international pageants, such as the Miss International Contest.

Contestants line up at the Tenth Annual Grandma Bathing Beauty Contest in 1941.

taking advantage of starstruck children . . . or starstruck parents. Pageants lost popularity and television coverage declined. As a result, advertisers were slow to support shows. It was, says Griff O'Neil, president of IPA, a crisis in the industry.

Some pageants do take advantage of the dreams of young girls . . . and of older women. O'Neil urges contestlants to ask if an event is approved by the IPA. If not, those who want to enter should ask for information on rules and regulations, prizes, and judges. If a pageant is honest and respectable, its organizers will clearly state the rewards of competing in it. Others, however, make vague promises, such as one pageant that guaranteed "that

Hopeful parents wait with their children backstage at a baby pageant.

the event would be broadcast on national television and that winners would appear in a video "for consideration to be a contestant on Star Search." All it really offered was that the winners would be considered. A magazine advertisement for another pageant said, "Pageant will be videotaped for television." There was no guarantee that a television network would use the video.

IPA produces a newsletter, *Winning*, which publishes articles by such stars as Garth Brooks (an IPA member) and information about modeling and health concerns. In a typical issue one article warned of the dangers of anorexia, an eating disorder, and another discussed how fingernails are an indicator of health.

There are also several independent magazines, including *Pageantry, Pageant Life Magazine,* and *Pageant Update.* They carry news of major state competitions that can lead a contestant to Miss America, Miss United States, or Miss USA titles. They also describe less well-known competitions, such as Mrs. All Nations of America, which advertises that it celebrates today's modern woman and needs state directors.

Advertisements in these magazines indicate how big the pageant business has become. There are ads for specialists in cosmetic surgery (nose jobs, liposuction, and more), and cosmetic dentistry; and for wardrobe designers who provide interview suits and dresses, competition swimsuits, jewelry, shoes, accessories, and gowns for the final coronation event. Pageant photographers offer their services, to take pictures of individual contestants for their personal promotion packages. A family grooming a child for pageant competition can spend a lot of money on these services—and much more on talent training. Some contestants come to the contest with more than twelve years of training in piano, dance, or in whatever field their talent may be.

How-to publications are available for those who want to enter a contest. There is an *International Directory of Pageants* ($50), a tape entitled *"The Power to Win"* by a former pageant judge, and a book, *101 Secrets to Winning Beauty Pageants.* No one needs to enter a contest unprepared, although some observers criticize this training and preparation. The true Miss America, they claim, should excel as she is, without training and the services of makeup, hairstyling, and other experts.

The number and variety of people involved in the pageant industry is another indication of how big a busi-

The young winner takes a bow after a children's pageant.

ness this is: event directors, contestants, future contestants, parents, families, friends, trainers, sponsors, advertisers, publishers, associations, media people.

The Miss America Pageant is always held in Atlantic City, New Jersey, but many other contests are moved from place to place. Cities are eager to host pageants because they attract tourists and business. When the Miss Universe Pageant was held in Cancun, Mexico, in 1990, that city had such an economic boom that it tried hard to get the contest to return. The pageant organizers, however, kept to their rotating schedule.

Because the Miss America pageant is the largest and has the longest history, it serves as a model for all other pageants. It is also the pageant, according to O'Neil, which started the modern industry of pageantry.

An international pageant brings attention and business to the host country. Here Nelson Mandela welcomes Miss World finalists to South Africa.

three

HISTORY OF THE MISS AMERICA PAGEANT

I n 1921, Atlantic City, New Jersey, was a popular tourist resort. In the summer people flocked there to sun and swim at the city's famous beaches, and to see and be seen on its famous Boardwalk. But city leaders wanted to help the tourist season last beyond Labor Day, to bring more business to the city. They came up with the idea of a Fall Pageant featuring many events, among them a bathing beauty contest on the beach.

Two newspaper writers suggested that newspapers along the East Coast sponsor young women for the bathing beauty contest. Readers could send photos of prospective contestants to the newspaper editors; the editors would choose the one they thought was the prettiest, and she would represent that paper's city in the Atlantic City contest. In the actual contest, a panel of artists was to select "the most beautiful bathing beauty in America." And someone had the idea to call the winner "Miss America."

*Contestants
in the first Miss
America contest, 1921*

The eight contestants in the first contest were divided into categories: there was one "professional" candidate — either a model or an actress; the others were "civic" and "inter-city" candidates. Washington, D.C., sent a young woman, as did the New Jersey cities of Camden, Ocean City, and Newark; Pennsylvania entries came from Pittsburgh, Harrisburg, and Philadelphia. The young women competed in several events, but the most popular was the "Bathers Revue" — huge crowds watched as they paraded along the beach in bathing suits.

Wearing a Statue of Liberty-style crown, the first Miss America, Margaret Gorman, receives an honorary key to Atlantic City from the mayor in 1921.

In those days there were strict rules about swimwear. Bathing suits were long tights, with a tunic or jersey on top, and a young woman might be arrested if her swimsuit was too revealing. Atlantic City had a law against bare arms or legs, but the law was relaxed just a bit for this contest, to the shock of some spectators. Still, today we would consider those bathing suits about equal to a sweatsuit . . . and 1921 spectators would be shocked at swimwear of the 1990s!

"King Neptune, the God of the Sea"—really an eighty-one-year-old inventor named Hudson Maxim—presided over the Boardwalk Rolling Chair Parade, which resembled a modern Thanksgiving Day parade with floats and bands. Airplanes flew overhead and dropped confetti on the crowd, and fireworks went off in midair. The beauty contestants rode in the rolling wicker chairs usually used by bathers on the Boardwalk.

Sixteen-year-old Margaret Gorman of Washington, D.C., was the first Miss America, crowned by "King Neptune." Her crown was a copy of the one worn by the Statue of Liberty, in New York Harbor, and her robe was fashioned from an American flag. She was given, for one year, a "Golden Mermaid" trophy said to be worth $5,000.

The first contest was a huge success—tourists extended their vacations, merchants increased their profits—and the city leaders voted to repeat the contest. In those days the queen could compete to keep her

King Neptune on the Atlantic City Boardwalk, flanked by the outgoing Miss America 1921 (right) and the newly crowned Miss America 1922

A poster announcing the 1923 pageant in Atlantic City

title for another year. Margaret Gorman was defeated by Mary Katherine Campbell of Ohio, who held the title in 1922 and 1923.

By the mid-1920s, the contest drew over seventy entries. It was not without problems: no one had thought to make a rule that contestants could not be married. It was a shock—and even considered a disgrace to the pageant—when it was revealed that several were indeed married and one had a baby. A number of women's clubs publicly called the contest "indecent." Faced with such criticism, officials canceled the pageant in 1928.

The contest was revived in 1933, but that year it lost money, due to several problems. Miss New York State collapsed on stage from an infected tooth; Miss Oklahoma was rushed to the hospital for an emergency appendectomy; Miss New York City dropped out; Miss Arkansas proved to be married; three other contestants were disqualified because they did not live in the states they represented; and one judge overslept, delaying the preliminary activities. A fifteen-year-old from Connecticut was crowned and held the title until 1935 when the next contest was held.

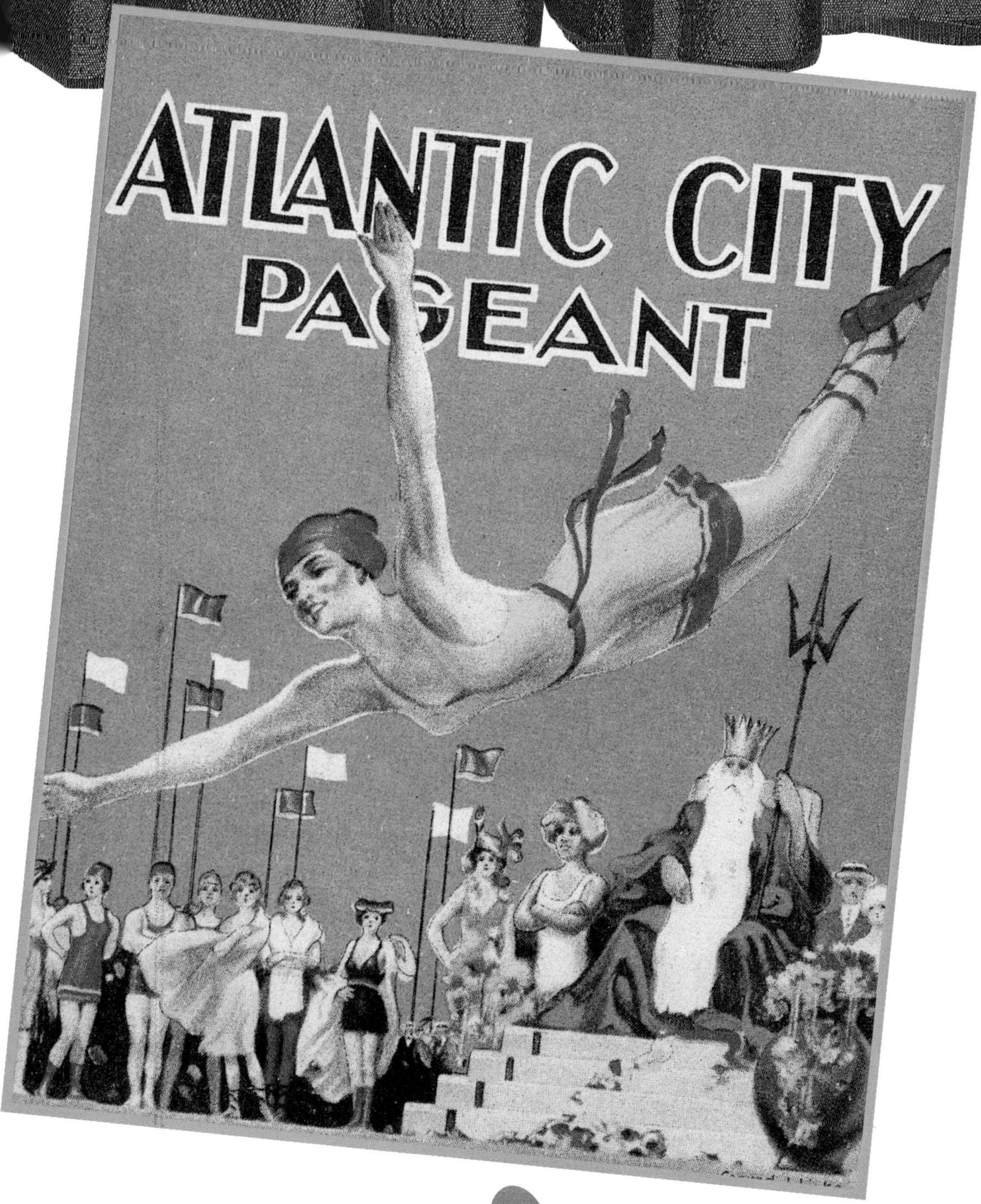
ATLANTIC CITY
PAGEANT

four

THE PAGEANT COMES BACK

T he successful revival of the pageant was due to one person: Leonora Slaughter, a Florida woman with experience as a civic events coordinator, who took the Atlantic City job "temporarily" and stayed thirty-two years. Some claim that Slaughter ruled with a heavy hand, making her preferences known to the judges, for instance, but she changed the show from a local pageant to a national institution. Slaughter first concentrated on getting the support of Atlantic City businesses and attracting the "finer" young women. No longer could anyone compete under the sponsorship of a newspaper or theater; only young women representing cities, regions, or states were allowed to enter. Contestants had to be between eighteen and twenty-one and never married. They were forbidden to enter bars or nightclubs during the pageant and had to be back in their rooms by 1:00 A.M. These rules still hold today, although contestants may be seventeen years old.

A talent competition was added. Although a talent act was not required, this competition for the first time

On the boardwalk at Steeplechase Park in New York City, young women compete for the crown of Miss Coney Island 1923 and the chance to go on to the Atlantic City Pageant.

put emphasis on something besides appearance. By the late 1930s, the talent competition was required, and the quality of the talent displayed improved a great deal.

Another crisis loomed when the 1937 winner ran away within hours of being crowned. She was, she later said, not ready to quit school and take on the responsibilities of being Miss America. The runaway had been aided in her escape by a young Atlantic City man who

A newsreel photographer records the events of the 1939 pageant, to be shown in movie theaters around the country.

had been assigned to her as an escort. From then on, each contestant was assigned a woman to act as her host and chaperone. The hosts were leading members of the community and were responsible for their charges every minute they were not onstage. Pageant candidates are probably the most closely watched and chaperoned young women in the country, even today.

There was no television, but by the late 1930s millions of Americans saw the annual pageant in newsreels in their local movie theaters. This made the pageant truly a national event.

World War II brought difficult times. Atlantic City was occupied by the military, its luxury hotels became barracks, and the convention hall, where the pageant was held, became a military training site. Blackouts—when all lights had to be turned off or hidden to confuse any possible enemy bombers—darkened the Boardwalk. The pageant continued, however, giving the country something to enjoy during the war years.

During the war years, many beauty pageant winners, including Miss America, worked in bond drives and other activities to support the nation's war effort.

During those years Leonora Slaughter built up a network of state and local contests to feed the pageant. If a young woman won a local contest, she moved on to her state contest. If she won that, she represented her state in the national contest. Today there are over 2,000 preliminary Miss America competitions from Hawaii to New England.

The scholarship program was begun in this period. In 1943, Jean Bartel, a student at the University of California at Los Angeles, was the first college student to win the title. There were few scholarships available for women then—although many existed for young men—and it was suggested that the pageant offer a scholarship. Leonora Slaughter handwrote 236 letters asking various companies to contribute to a scholarship fund: five responded. Miss

Bess Myerson, Miss America 1945, won the first pageant scholarship.

30

America 1945, Bess Myerson, a graduate of Hunter College in New York City, received the first scholarship. She used it for graduate studies at Columbia University.

The scholarship fund grew. By 1946 it was $25,000 and the winner shared it with fifteen national finalists. By 1950 the program had spread to the state and regional pageants. Today the Miss America pageant system awards $24 million in scholarships at the state and local level, and Miss America receives scholarship money of $35,000.

After the war, Atlantic City was again a vacation resort and the pageant

Leonora Slaughter, long-time director of the Miss America pageant, here presents a scholarship award to Miss Canada, 1947.

Local contests have awarded a variety of titles. Top left: Miss Poinsettia Queen is crowned in an underwater show. Center: Miss Posture Queen, in a contest where the judging was based on spinal X rays. Top right: For the title of Miss Beautiful Legs, contestants' heads were covered so that the judges would not be influenced by a beautiful face.

blossomed. A fourth standard, intelligence and personality, was added to the competition. And in 1948 the judges decided that for the final event—which ended in the coronation—the girls should wear evening gowns rather than swimsuits. It was another step away from the bathing beauty contest.

A disagreement about bathing suits is said to have led to the creation of the Miss USA pageant. The Catalina company, manufacturers of swimwear, had been featuring Miss America every year in a swimsuit style-show tour. The 1951 title holder, Yolande Betbeze, refused to model swimsuits and wanted appearances where she could use her training in opera. The pageant board of directors supported Miss Betbeze. Catalina promptly began its own pageant—Miss USA—as a means of advertising swimwear.

In 1954 the Miss America pageant was televised for the first time. Now people across the country could watch it live, instead of waiting to see a movie newsreel. About 27 million people tuned in that first night. Pageant officials had been afraid to allow the event to be televised in nearby Philadelphia, for fear people would stay home rather than buy tickets and come to the Atlantic City Convention Hall. Just the opposite happened: more people than ever showed up at the pageant.

The next year, Bert Parks was host and master of ceremonies of the pageant, a position he would hold for twenty-five years, firmly linking his name to that of the Miss America pageant. And that first year, Parks introduced the song "There She Is—Miss America!"

Bert Parks sings the annual theme song, "There She Is—Miss America," at the 1966 pageant.

33

five

CHANGES IN AMERICA, CHANGES IN THE PAGEANT

I n the 1960s and 1970s, the atmosphere in the United States changed dramatically. These were the years of the Vietnam War and of the beginnings of the women's and civil rights movements. They were difficult years for the pageant; for the first time there were accusations that it took advantage of young women.

In 1968 protestors picketed the pageant. Women marched chanting antipageant slogans and threw makeup, hair curlers, and women's underwear into a "freedom trash can." They refused to talk with male reporters, and they invaded the final ceremony and threw a stink bomb onto the famous runway.

The years when protestors attacked the pageant as a girlie parade were, however, years in which Miss America 1974, Rebecca King of Colorado, earned a law degree and Miss America 1975, Shirley Cothran of Texas, went on to earn a doctorate in education. Clearly, the women

Demonstrators protest the 1968 Miss America Pageant as degrading to women.

had moved beyond swimsuits, whether the protestors recognized it or not.

The pageant was also criticized for failing to recognize minorities. The bylaws stated that the pageant was open to all races, but nearly all contestants were Anglos. Many minority women entered regional contests, but none had made it to the national finals until 1970, when Cheryl Browne, an African-American, was named Miss Iowa.

In 1983 the first African-American Miss America was crowned—Vanessa Williams, who reigned for ten months as one of the pageant's most popular queens until a scandal involving nude photographs erupted. Williams resigned in favor of the runner-up, Suzette Charles, who became the second black Miss America. Williams went on to a career in television and films, and the pageant has survived that and other scandals, such as the accusation

that a winner had had a "nose job."

In 1989 the ten pageant finalists included a hearing-impaired classical pianist, an organ transplant recipient, an African-American, and two Asian-Americans, statistics which should counter the charge that the pageant wants only "perfect" Anglo candidates. The crown went to Miss Missouri, Debbye Turner, the third black Miss America.

In the 1990s, the pageant continues to grow and change, leaving behind its image as a bathing beauty contest. Entrants now write an essay on social issues of particular concern to them and are encouraged to adopt a "platform" stating their position, much like a political platform. Titleholders have spoken for such causes as eliminating homelessness, prevention of violence against children, medical research, and youth motivation. In 1994, the first woman with a disability was elected—Heather Whitestone, who is hearing-impaired. The cause she championed was education for the hearing-impaired. (Since 1950, a year in which there was no contest, the queen elected one year is the official queen for the next year: Miss Whitestone was elected Miss America 1995 in 1994.)

Contestants are now interviewed onstage, without knowing the questions ahead of time. This is to demonstrate their understanding of current issues. And in a high-tech development, Miss America 1995 orbited in cyberspace. The computer network America On-Line featured Heather Whitestone on-line for three days. Customers could call up on their computers photos and biographies of contestants for the next title.

The 1994 pageant also saw a major change in the swimsuit competition. Competitors kicked off their high heels to walk barefoot during the swimsuit part of the program, which was an entertainment number with a beach background instead of the traditional parade up and down the runway. The change led

Heather Whitestone is crowned Miss America, 1995.

Miss America contestants rehearse the opening production number in the pageant in front of television cameras.

to less emphasis on the young women as sex objects, a charge often leveled at the pageant.

The 1990s also saw increases in scholarship funding—a Fruit of the Loom "Quality of Life" program awards $60,000 to young women whose volunteer work improves life in their communities; a $10,000 Women's Achievement Award goes to outstanding American women whose volunteer work has benefited society— recipients include former First Ladies Betty Ford and Rosalynn Carter for work with alcohol recovery programs, breast cancer, and mental health; a $10,000 contribution is made by the pageant to the winner's college to assist female students.

THE CONTESTANTS

When Margaret Gorman was named the first Miss America, she had no special training for the contest and may well have entered it on a whim. Over the years, other women have unexpectedly found themselves candidates—Lee Meriwether (1955) was entered into the Miss San Francisco Pageant by a fraternity president when she skipped a joint fraternity-sorority meeting, and Marilyn Van Derbur (1958) was drafted by her sorority when she left a meeting for a phone call.

But most contestants have prepared for years to earn a chance at national competition. Many take modeling lessons and other training to improve their self-confidence as well as their posture. They learn interview techniques, how to style their hair and makeup, how to choose their wardrobe. And they spend years developing their talent.

Judith Ford (1968) took professional modeling lessons to prepare for the national competition after she won the Miss Illinois contest. When her instructor said that she walked like an athlete—she performed on the trampoline for her talent requirement—she said, "Thank you." "No, no!" said the instructor, "that's not a compliment."

The talent portion of the show has led to surprises. One might expect musical presentations—voice, piano,

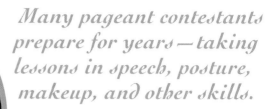

Many pageant contestants prepare for years—taking lessons in speech, posture, makeup, and other skills.

violin—and theatrical acts. In recent years, however, in addition to Ford's trampoline routine, winners have presented ventriloquism acts, comedy routines, a mock striptease (outlawed after one performance), and a Hawaiian-Tahitian dance. Miss America candidates are creative in their selection of talents to develop and nurture.

The road to a crown begins with a local pageant, usually for the title of queen of a city—Miss Springfield or Miss Abilene or Miss Colorado Springs. The young women must apply and be accepted as candidates; across the country about 80,000 young women enter local contests. After acceptance and some "get acquainted" parties, the rehearsal process begins. The actual judging includes private interviews and a one-evening competition with three events—talent, swimsuit, and evening gown. In a mini-version of the Atlantic City pageant, the winner is crowned with a tiara, congratulated by family and fellow contestants, and surrounded by photographers. Almost immediately, she is whisked away to begin preparing for the state pageant.

Once a young woman wins a contest that is part of a major pageant network, she has the aid and encouragement of officials within that network. They give pointers on the best part of her performance and suggestions for improving other areas. They may help with the arrangement of musical scores for the talent competition, advise on an evening gown, encourage a makeup makeover, do

Students in a pageant training class rehearse their reactions to being named a contest winner.

whatever may help the contestant win. After all, local officials want their candidate to reign over her state and
finally the nation. In fact, the suggestion is often made
that state judges select not the most talented or most artic-
ulate entrant but the one they think has the best chance
of winning, the one that looks like a Miss America. That
thought supports the idea that all contestants are basi-
cally cut from one mold.

State contests, in the late spring or early summer, narrow the field of over 2,000 local title-holders to 50 winners. In some states, these pageants are almost local
holidays, lasting a week and involving hundreds of vol-
unteers and lots of community support. The week, pat-
terned after the national pageant, is hectic, filled with
rehearsals, public appearances, photo sessions, receptions,
and television tapings.

A state title involves more responsibilities, so winners

*Finalists in a state
contest hope for a
chance to move on
and compete in
a national
pageant.*

Despite the hardships of travel, these contestants in an international pageant keep smiling.

frequently take a year off from school or career to make public appearances. They earn a good income from these appearances and often get free shopping sprees, complimentary automobiles, cruises, jewelry—and, of course, scholarships. But they must put up with some difficulties—constant travel, the need to be always up and smiling for the public, requests for speeches, autographs, and photos. No matter how tired they are or how long they've been traveling, they must look bright, happy, and enthusiastic. In many ways, it's a difficult year.

Despite other responsibilities, state winners devote the summer to preparing for the national contest. Cheryl

Prewitt (1980) worked hard the summer before her contest. After being named Miss Mississippi, she moved in with state officials who designed a tough program for her. She was up at 6:30 A.M. for a three-hour exercise workout; then she studied newspaper and television news; after a break for lunch and sunbathing came more exercise and more study. A light dinner was followed by practice in pivoting, working with microphones, timing her talent act, and videotaping mock interviews. The day ended at 11:00 P.M. with a final hour of exercise. This lasted for at least three months.

By contrast, a spokesperson for the Miss United States pageant says that by the time a contestant wins a state title, she is in "pretty good shape." Fixing makeup or hair is a matter only of hours, though the contestants have to learn to do it themselves because they travel so much. Beyond that, she says, training is a question of working with young women individually to improve specific areas—perhaps interview techniques, speech, or posture.

A Miss USA contestant gets some hair-styling assistance before the pageant.

seven

THE PAGEANT

T he national pageant is the climax to years of preparation. In many ways, it is a more intense version
of what the young women have already experi-
enced at the state level — but the contest is in Atlantic City
and the stakes are higher. Accompanied by family, friends,
and official chaperones, the young women arrive in
Atlantic City a week before the pageant. Again their days
are filled with rehearsals and interviews with newspaper
and television journalists.

The parade which began the pageant tradition in 1921
is still a part of the event, although contestants don't wear
bathing suits and don't ride in rolling boardwalk chairs.
Instead, they wear elaborate gowns and ride in automobiles. Still, thousands of people turn out to see them, and
they feel like celebrities.

Next there are the preliminary competitions — talent,
evening gown, and swimsuit. The fifty contestants rotate
through these competitions, but they always begin with
a private interview with the judges. The judges ask timely
questions — in 1996, it might have been about the
Olympics. It puts the contestants at ease to see that the

The traditional Boardwalk Parade in 1925

judges are everyday people and not monsters waiting to trip them up, although one criticism of the pageant is that the judges are indeed ordinary people—with no training for judging contestants.

Pageant Day is hectic and exciting, but most of it is spent rehearsing—production numbers, the parade of states, the announcement of the top ten, the court of honor, and the crowning of Miss America. In the dressing rooms as everyone prepares for the 8:00 P.M. pageant, the tension level is high—and it gets higher as the ceremony begins with the introduction of the contestants, the reigning queen, and the judges.

The announcement of the ten finalists is a bittersweet moment. Each contestant longs to be named, and for those who are not, the disappointment is great. Fortunately all contestants are involved in production numbers, so the forty non-finalists are kept busy. The ten finalists, meanwhile, fly through the pageant at a hectic pace, changing for talent events, production numbers, and evening gown competition, which includes an interview. An army of women stand ready to help with hooks, buttons, zippers, hair, makeup, and nerves. Many girls, both finalists and not, report that just being there is the most important part of the evening.

The moment when Miss America is crowned is emotional. One by one the runners-up are named, until six contestants are left standing on the stage, each wondering if she is the winner. When the new Miss America is named, the winner often buries her head in her hands or

Pageants now often include elaborate production numbers such as this scene from the Miss World pageant.

in some other way gives in to her overpowering feelings. But then she is crowned, handed flowers, and expected to walk down the runway into the audience. Some winners have remembered the loneliness of the moment — they are no longer one of fifty contestants but are out there on that runway alone. Phyllis George in 1970 had perhaps the most embarrassing moment: her crown fell and she had to carry it in her hand. Whatever their experience, it is a moment the winners — and their fans — long remember.

The moment of winning brings forth a variety of reactions. Here a contestant reacts to being named Miss Universe.

eight

A YEAR AS QUEEN

For those contestants who did not win, it's back home to finish out the year as the state queen. And almost always it's on to career and professional accomplishments. Here are a few of the things former contestants went on to do: one became a lawyer and assistant district attorney; another is a physician who lectures on diseases of the eye; Cloris Leachman became an actress and won four Emmy Awards and an Academy Award; Joan Blondell, Dorothy L'Amour, Susan Anton, and Delta Burke also became successful actresses; Anita Bryant became a well-known singer and commercial spokesperson. The list is long.

But what about Miss America? In a sense, the year as queen is a letdown. For most contestants, the goal was not to spend a year touring the country making public appearances; it was to be crowned queen. Their thoughts rarely went beyond the coronation.

The year of touring, too, is something for which most contestant are unprepared. They have been trained to participate in a pageant, not to make nonstop public appearances while living out of a suitcase and trying hard to be always pretty and charming.

The queen must always be ready with a smile for photographers and the public.

From her coronation to the end of her reign, Miss America's days are filled with interviews, press conferences, photo sessions, and appearances.

Miss America's reign begins almost immediately after coronation with a press conference, and the pace never slows. The first day is filled with more press conferences, photo sessions, and appointments. Then it's off to New

York for an appearance on a morning television news program. Then there are more radio and television interviews and press conferences.

During the year Miss America makes about 200 public appearances and travels over 200,000 miles. In one month she may visit Houston, New York, Portland, Chicago, Indianapolis, Detroit, Philadelphia. She makes appearances for a wide variety of products, even cars and home appliances. She attends state fairs, sporting events, parades, and exhibits. She tours factories and attends museum openings, and she is ready with a smile anywhere a celebrity is needed. Her schedule is arranged by a business manager who tries to plan an occasional free day for rest. An official travel companion takes care of such details as lost luggage so that Miss America can concentrate on her public appearances. Usually at least two travel companions take turns traveling with Miss America; the schedule is too hard for one person to handle for a year.

Sometimes things go haywire — one Miss America had to climb out of the sunroof of her limousine when the doors were stuck, another had her gown ripped by an escalator, and Marilyn Van Derbur (1958) fell down a flight of stairs, with the spotlight on her, at the homecoming ceremony in Colorado.

Beauty pageant contestants make appearances at the host city's tourist attractions, such as Wichita's historic "Cowtown."

In spite of the strain of travel and always being on view, most who wear the crown report that the year goes by too quickly and is an unforgettable experience.

nine

AND AFTERWARD

Like the contestants she edged out in the finals, Miss America goes on to career and professional accomplishments. Recent crown-holders have studied law, veterinary medicine, and nursing; they have graduated from Ivy League schools, earned Phi Beta Kappa keys, danced with the Rockettes, married and started families. Among earlier winners, there are familiar names — Bess Myerson (1945) became a television journalist and consumer advocate; Lee Ann Meriwether (1955) appeared in the television series "Barnaby Jones" and "The Munsters Today" and was nominated for the Emmy and the Golden Globe awards; Mary Ann Mobley (1959) has appeared on "Different Strokes" and "Falcon Crest" and filmed documentaries in Cambodia and Africa; Phyllis George has coanchored "CBS Morning News" and more recently developed a gourmet chicken firm, Chicken by George; Vanessa Williams (1984) has appeared in several television programs, a TV movie, and three feature films and a few years ago earned two Grammy nominations with her first album.

The pageants are still often criticized as lacking meaning for the way America lives today. Some critics suggest that they show nothing more important than someone's ability to win a beauty contest. But being Miss America or Miss USA or Miss United States is not a goal in itself— it's preparation for life, says one Miss United States adviser who adds, "We put them on the road, in new situations, in press interviews, to raise their self-confidence and get them ready for the future so they can be good accountants, teachers, doctors, whatever. It's a matter of self-esteem."

Pageant contestants in the Miss International contest (right), the Miss USA contests, and the many other competitions around the world can gain knowledge, self-esteem, and a broader view of the future.

Pageant Terms

boardwalk — a wooden, planked walkway, usually on a beach; in the United States, the term "The Boardwalk" generally refers to the famous vacation site at Atlantic City, New Jersey

chaperone — a person, usually an older or married woman, who is responsible for the safety and proper behavior of a younger, unmarried woman; or one who attends a party of young people to oversee behavior

coronation — the act or ceremony of crowning a king, queen, or other royal person

finalist — a person who is chosen out of a large group of contestants to take part in the final round of a contest or competition

runway — a narrow walkway extending from a stage out into the audience; traditionally beauty queens walk down the runway immediately after they are crowned

tiara — a jeweled headpiece resembling a crown

For More Information

Ann-Marie Bivans's fascinating history, *Miss America, In Pursuit of the Crown* (New York: Master Media, Limited) gives a thorough picture of the Miss America Pageant and is recommended for those who want more details and information.

Frank DeFord's *There She Is — the Life and Times of Miss America* (New York: The Viking Press, 1971) gives a very different — but equally informative — view of the Miss America pageant.

Interested readers might consult *How to Win a Beauty Pageant* (Phoenix: Curan Publishing, 1960) by Jacq Mercer, Miss America 1949.

Information about other pageants may be found in pageantry magazines such as *Pageantry, Pageant Life Magazine, Pageant Update,* and the IPA newsletter, *Winning.*

Index

Page numbers in *italics* indicate illustrations.

About the Author

Judy Alter is the author of several dozen books for children, including *Women of the Old West*, *The Comanches*, *Rodeos: The Greatest Show on Dirt*, and *Wild West Shows: Rough Riders and Sure Shots* for Franklin Watts. She is the director of Texas Christian University Press, which publishes literature and history of Texas and the American West. Ms. Alter lives in Fort Worth, Texas.